GEORGE ANTHEIL

Sonata No. 2 for Violin and Piano

edited by Ron Erickson

ED-3994

First Printing: September 1995

Cover: "The Crowd" by Wyndham Lewis

Tate Gallery, London/Art Resource, NY

G. SCHIRMER, Inc.

DISTRIBUTED BY

HAL•LEONARD®
CORPORATION
7777 W. BLUEMOUND RD. P.O. BOX 13819 MILWAUKEE, WI 53213

The Works for Violin and Piano

Of the American composers who associated with the avant garde in Paris in the 1920s, George Antheil was the only one who may correctly be regarded as a modernist. Arriving in Europe in 1922 for a concert tour, the 22-year-old pianist soon came to be known for his futuristic compositions, which he included with new works by Schoenberg and other European composers on his otherwise conventional programs.

In his 1945 autobiography, Antheil reminisces that in 1923 Ezra Pound commissioned from him two sonatas as a vehicle for Pound's companion, the noted Irish-American violinist Olga Rudge. Inspired by Rudge's wild and intense artistry, Antheil produced both sonatas inside of four months. This period included a visit to Tunis in order to refresh his creative energies after completing the first movement of the First Sonata, from which he returned determined to get beyond its "Les Noces" sound.

To whatever extent Antheil succeeded in this, the modernistic devices in the Sonata No. 1 went well beyond Stravinsky's idiom. Antheil's tone clusters, complex irrational meters, additive silence, and distortion of timbre had first appeared in America around 1915 in the music of Henry Cowell and Leo Ornstein, but Antheil had to invent notations for such techniques for which, though they are now part of the general music vocabulary, there is still no standardized notation.

In the present edition, some of Antheil's rather homespun markings are replaced by ones more readily apparent to the performer, such as the hand with marked palm in bar 247 of Sonata No. 1 and note-head blocks for tone clusters, a notation invented by Cowell.

Where Stravinsky would use sequences of small meters of uneven length, Antheil used long bars with fractional rhythm values—producing an effect not too dissimilar from the East European meters associated with Bulgarian folk music. Single-digit meters are not qualitative, as in compound meters, but quantitative, in which the small rhythms are not grouped. This additive technique is the rational for Stravinsky's odd-numbered meters, and Antheil commented on it in his own music.

The upside-down down-bow mark was a convention at the time of this Sonata. It is retained here because of its association with "au talon," to convey some of the percussive spirit of the work to the performer.

The Sonata No. 1 was engraved and published in a reasonably credible edition during Antheil's stay in Paris. The Sonata No. 2 was never engraved or copied. According to Antheil's program for this brief, stormy work, an encapsulation of his point-to-point form, the "banal" popular music of the violin struggles with the modern music of the piano, culminating in a self-destructive tango cadenza that gives way to a quiet Arabian-style coda, perhaps Antheil's tribute to the "vast Mohammedan repertory" he discovered in Tunis in 1923.

George Antheil's Sonata No. 3 (1924) is the last of the group of three written during the composer's association with the Paris scene of the 1920s. It is the most cohesive in form and the most consistent in the idiom associated with Stravinsky in those years.

The notation sources for this edition of the Sonata No. 3 include photocopies of a manuscript score, titled in French, currently in the Library of Congress, and a fair copy of the violin part apparently made from that score. The score contains a number of small changes made in a large and hurried hand which appear to relate to performances, including a direction, in German, to turn the violinist's page. A few bars are crossed out to avoid repetition of material, for instance, mm. 130–167. At m. 250 is the direction "now cut back to Sonata I, IV," dated 1943. Antheil may have consolidated the first and third sonatas in performance, as he did when he listed his works the following year. Several pages, including from m. 359 to the end, are in Antheil's hand.

Antheil may with some justification be described as one of the earliest American modernists in music after Charles Ives. His musical style, both original and reflective of the new influences of his time, points in several directions. Perhaps, since he was usually the pianist in performances of his sonatas, consistent grammar of notation and a thorough marking of dynamics and expression seems not to have been a primary concern for him. Hence, actual errors and omissions in the score, some more obvious than others, are difficult to identify and resolve.

As with many composers, Antheil expressed his consternation about well-meaning "corrections" made by copyists dismayed by his dissonant writing. Where passages give rise to questions, a judicious choice is attempted here, tested by eye and ear, between likely assumptions, where changes are not identified, and reasonable doubt. Additions and suggestions, such as dynamics, are given in brackets, and changes are footnoted with reference to the original (indicated by "orig."). Markings that appear to have been added for performances are enclosed in the present edition by parentheses. These markings are sometimes at variance with the copyist's indications, suggesting the degree to which artistic preferences may override the composer's indications. Recapitulations of opening passages do not include all the earlier markings. Most of these differences are left here for the artist to resolve.

Modern notation conventions have been adapted to Antheil's chromatic-polytonal language in order to make the text as definite and as readable as possible. In this edition, polytonal key signatures sometimes are substituted for masses of accidentals. Accidentals in each hand are independent of the other hand, but support octave cross-relations, cancellations, and confirmations within the line. Where these may still be missing, the artist must decide the solution. Ambiguities are noted where deemed appropriate. A particular problem is the use in the original of a flat where a sharp or natural would seem more fitting. Such questions are part of the immediate energy that Antheil's music still inspires.

As a clue to the sound Antheil had in mind for three sonatas of the 1920s, it may help to consider his description, in his 1945 autobiography *Bad Boy of Music*, of the violinist he worked with in Paris, Olga Rudge, the companion of Ezra Pound: ". . . a consummate violinist. I have heard many violinists, but none with the superb lower register of the D and G strings that was Olga's exclusively."

After writing three sonatas for violin and piano in the early 1920s for the concerts promoted by Ezra Pound and Virgil Thomson in Paris, Antheil explored other means of expressing his music, such as opera. Like so many other artists, he settled in Hollywood in the late 1930s, thereafter to lead the double life of movie score writer and concert composer. He wrote his fourth and fifth works for violin and piano in the mid–1940s.

Whereas the early sonatas drew inspiration primarily from the Stravinsky style of that time, the later works show the influence of Prokofiev and Shostakovich, who had become primary models for all film composers. Antheil wrote the Sonatina in 1945 for the German violinist Werner Gebauer, concertmaster of the Dallas Symphony, who also played Antheil's Violin Concerto. Gebauer premiered the Sonatina in New York with great success.

Sonata No. 4, completed three years later, was entitled "No. 2" by Antheil. It appears, from the list of works he made in 1944, that of the works from the Paris years he wanted to consolidate the Sonata No. 1 with the Third and ignore the Second, so that all the violin and piano sonatas before 1940 would be known as one work, called Sonata No. 1.

Antheil regarded the Hollywood sonatas as evidence of his contrapuntal interest, departing from the rhythmic preoccupation of the 1920s. Certainly he had in mind a different kind of violinist as well, the virtuosic Heifetz variety (although Heifetz did not play Antheil's music). Just as the early works retain the appeal of their somewhat primal vigor to the present, the later works sparkle with sophisticated humor, brilliant energy, and charm with their long, singing lines.

The sources for this edition of Sonata No. 4 include a score in Antheil's hand and a violin part by a copyist. Numerous but superficial discrepancies, ambiguities, and inconsistencies have been variously resolved, noted, or accepted here, as seemed appropriate. The cuts in the score may only be performance options. They are not indicated in the copyist's violin part but are observed in the excellent recording by Israel Baker and Yaltah Menuhin.

One curious marking is the "greater-than" or "less-than" hairpin in front of a new dynamic level, taken by the editor to indicate the direction of dynamic change. Though this marking is not always clearly distinguishable in the manuscript from a regular crescendo or diminuendo, it is retained here as a useful notation to the performer, and an example of the composer's characteristically imaginative solutions to all kinds of problems.

—RON ERICKSON

for Ezra Pound, best of friends

SONATA No. 2

George Antheil

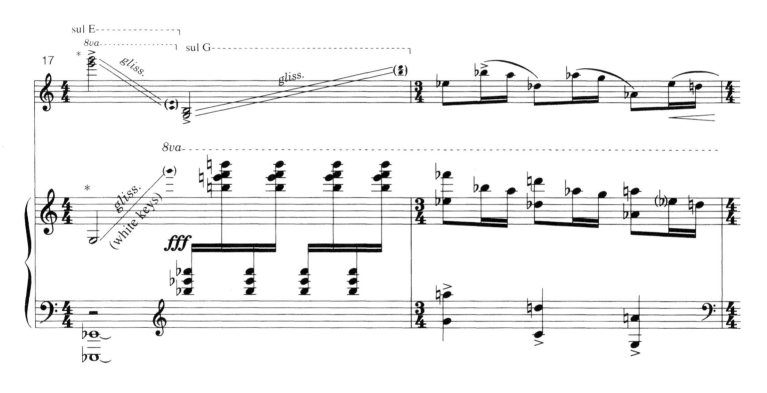

* the length of the *glissandi* is only approximate.

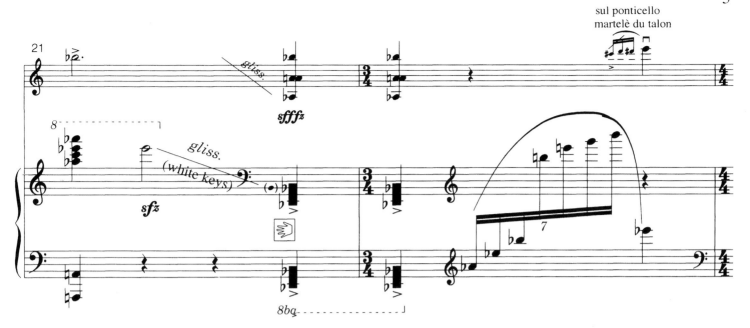

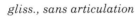

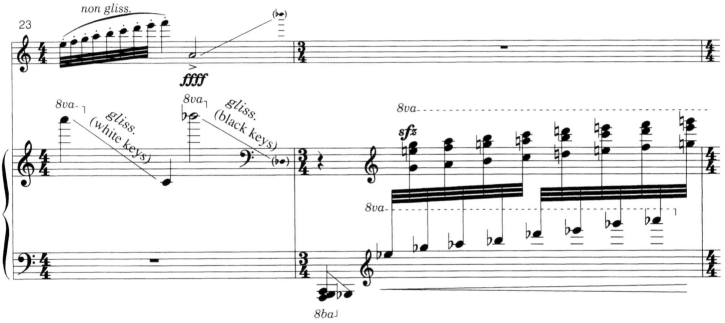

4

giggled
up near the tip of the bow

pizz.

arco

twice as fast

very lyric—a little "off"

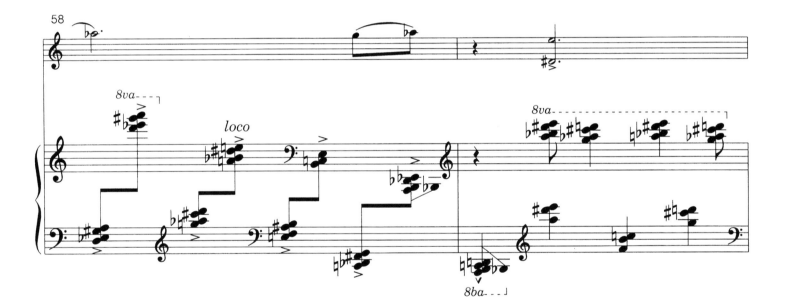

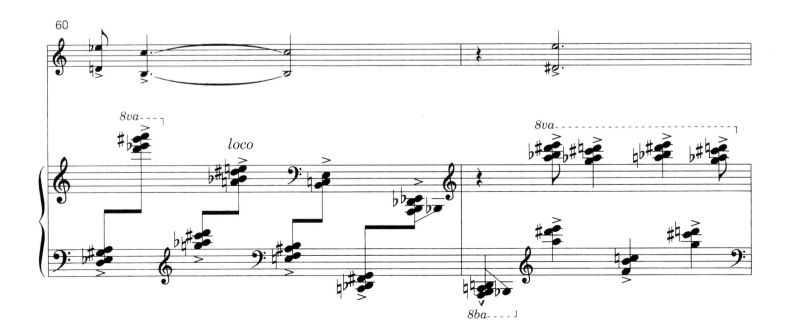

hurried but sweet

up to the minute
loco
pizz.

10 **Presto** (♪ = ♩)

Slow (♩ = ♪)
romantic (sweet)

sour

suddenly **fff**

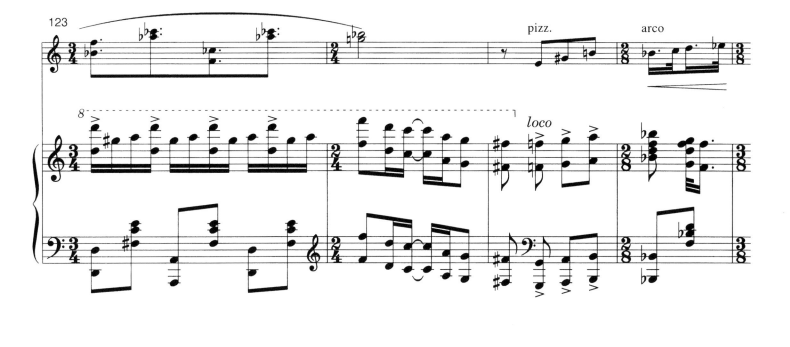

Slower, *church organ like*

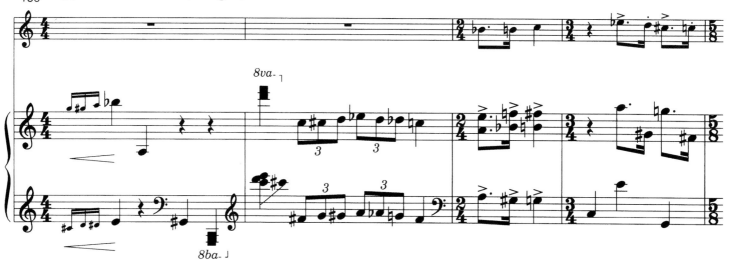

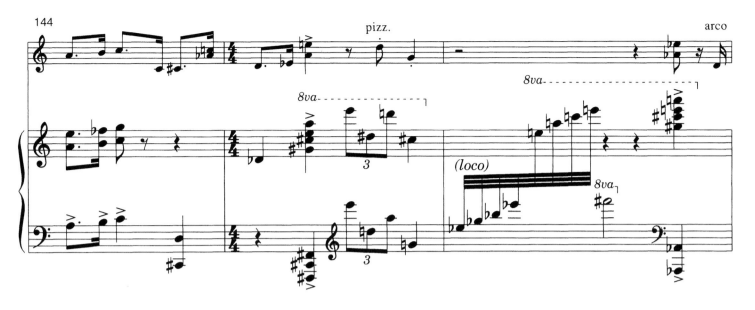

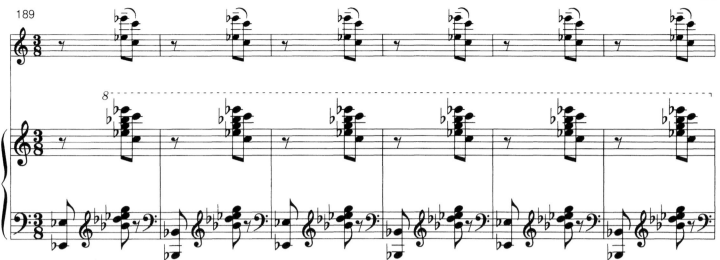

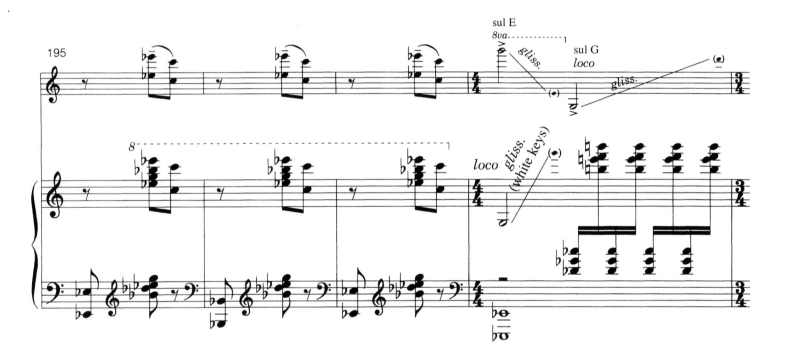

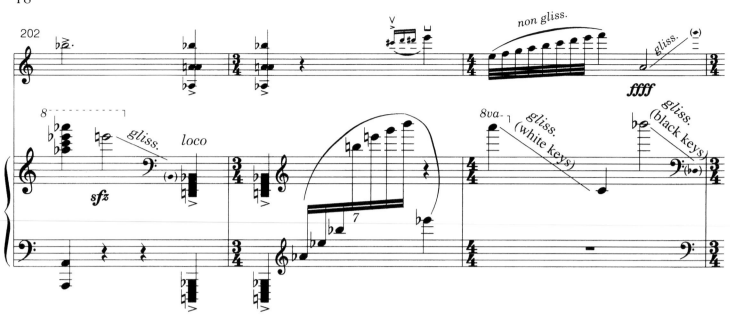

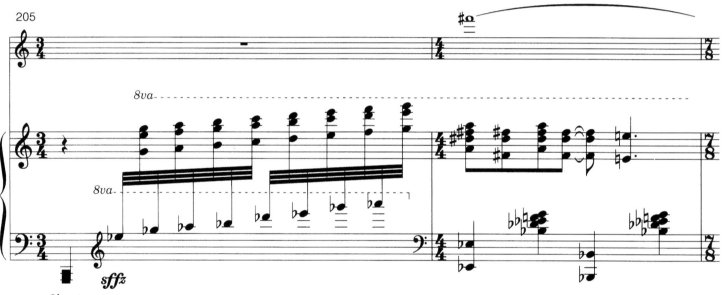

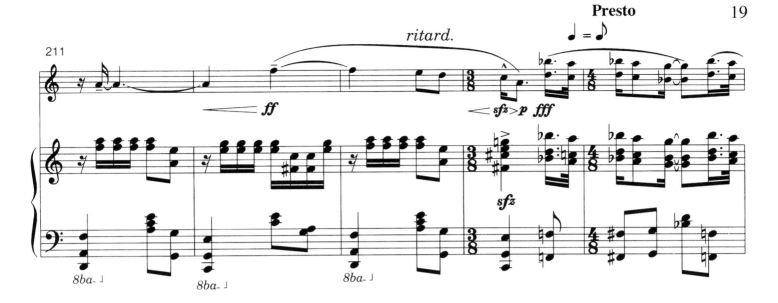

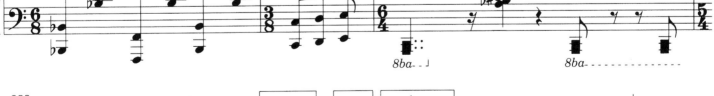

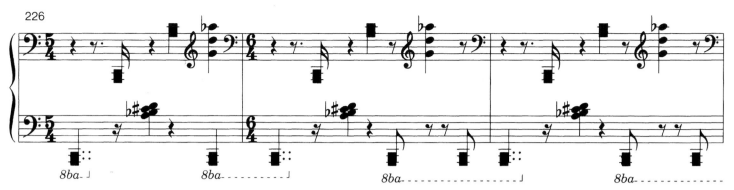

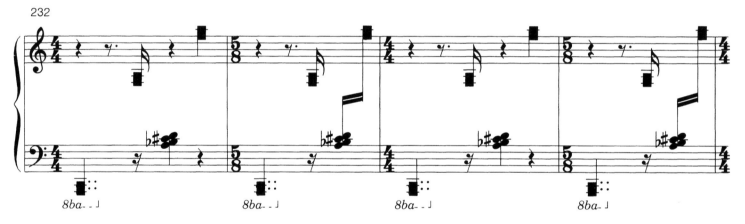

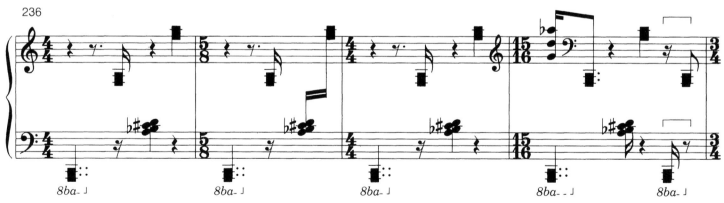

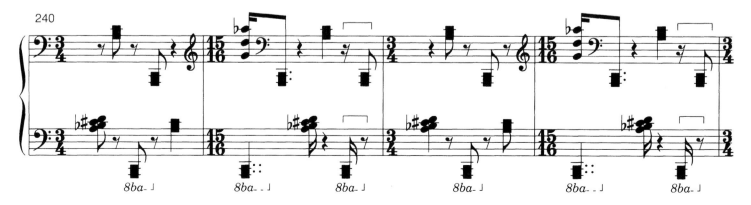

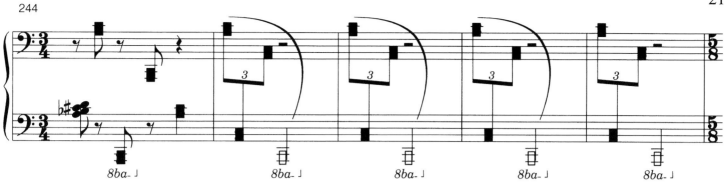

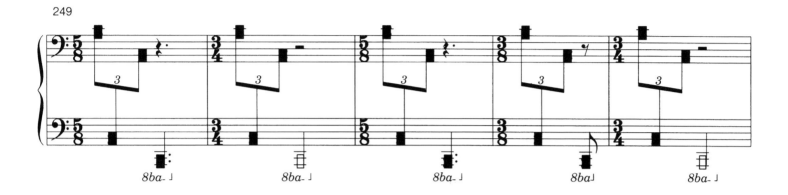

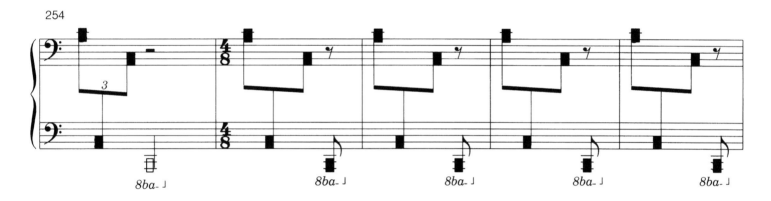

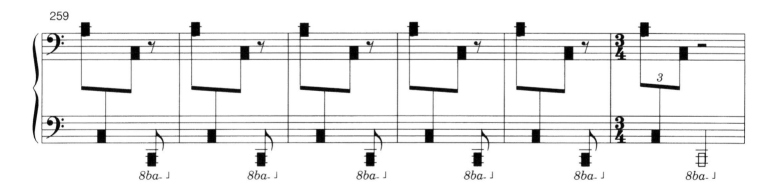

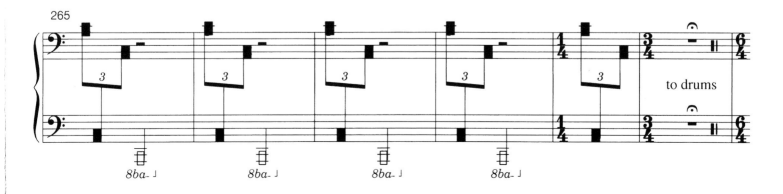

271

tenor drum

bass drum

275

278

281

283

286

290

294

GEORGE ANTHEIL

Sonata No. 2 for Violin and Piano

edited by Ron Erickson

Violin

ED-3994

First Printing: September 1995

Cover: "The Crowd" by Wyndham Lewis

Tate Gallery, London/Art Resource, NY

G. SCHIRMER, Inc.

DISTRIBUTED BY

HAL•LEONARD®
CORPORATION

7777 W. BLUEMOUND RD. P.O. BOX 13819 MILWAUKEE, WI 53213

for Ezra Pound, best of friends
SONATA No. 2

Edited by Ron Erickson

George Antheil

* The length of the glissando is only approximate.

** Longer slurs, such as this one, are phrasings, not bowings.

suddenly sour

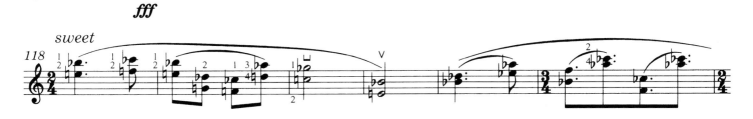

sweet

snappy

Slower, church organ like   Slow

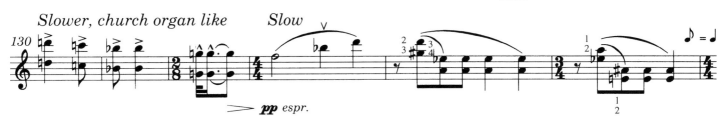

doppio movimento (allegro)